Homemade Protein Bar Recipes to Accelerate Muscle Development for Weightlifting:

Naturally improve muscle growth and lower fat to lift more and recover faster

By

Joseph Correa

Certified Sports Nutritionist

COPYRIGHT

© 2016 Finibi Inc

All rights reserved

Reproduction or translation of any part of this work beyond that permitted by section 107 or 108 of the 1976 United States Copyright Act without the permission of the copyright owner is unlawful.

This publication is designed to provide accurate and authoritative information in regard to

The subject matter covered. It is sold with the understanding that neither the author nor the publisher is engaged in rendering medical advice. If medical advice or assistance is needed, consult with a doctor. This book is considered a guide and should not be used in any way detrimental to your health. Consult with a physician before starting this nutritional plan to make sure it's right for you.

ACKNOWLEDGEMENTS

The realization and success of this book could not have been possible without my family.

Homemade Protein Bar Recipes to Accelerate Muscle Development for Weightlifting:

Naturally improve muscle growth and lower fat to lift more and recover faster

By

Joseph Correa

Certified Sports Nutritionist

Homemade Protein Bar Recipes to Accelerate Muscle Development for Weightlifting

CONTENTS

Copyright

Acknowledgements

About The Author

Introduction

Homemade Protein Bar Recipes to Accelerate Muscle Development for Weightlifting

Other Great Titles by This Author

ABOUT THE AUTHOR

As a certified sports nutritionist and professional athlete, I firmly believe that proper nutrition will help you reach your goals faster and effectively. My knowledge and experience has helped me live healthier throughout the years and which I have shared with family and friends. The more you know about eating and drinking healthier, the sooner you will want to change your life and eating habits.

Being successful in controlling your weight is important as it will improve all aspects of your life.

Nutrition is a key part in the process of getting in better shape and that's what this book is all about.

INTRODUCTION

Homemade Protein Bar Recipes to Accelerate Muscle Development for Weightlifting: Naturally improve muscle growth and lower fat to lift more and recover faster

This book will help you increase the amount of protein you consume per day to help increase muscle mass. These meals will help increase muscle in an organized manner by adding large healthy portions of protein to your diet. Being too busy to eat right can sometimes become a problem and that's why this book will save you time and help nourish your body to achieve the goals you want. Make sure you know what you're eating by preparing it yourself or having someone prepare it for you.

This book will help you to:

-Gain muscle fast naturally.

-Improve muscle recovery faster than usual.

-Eat delicious food that will improve performance.

Homemade Protein Bar Recipes to Accelerate Muscle Development for Weightlifting

-Have more energy during and after training.

-Naturally accelerate Your Metabolism to build more muscle.

-Improve your digestive system.

Joseph Correa is a certified sports nutritionist and a professional athlete.

HOMEMADE PROTEIN BAR RECIPES TO ACCELERATE MUSCLE DEVELOPMENT FOR WEIGHTLIFTING

1. Chocolate protein bars

Ingredients:

1 cup of oat flakes

3 scoops of protein powder – chocolate flavor

3 tbsp of peanut butter (choose organic peanut butter)

1.5 cup of skim milk

2 tbsp of brown sugar

Preparation:

Chocolate protein bars are very easy to prepare. They are healthy and tasty at the same time. Mix the ingredients until you get a slightly sticky mass. Be patient – this might take some time (approximately 15 minutes). Use containers for chocolate bars (if you don't have these, cream cheese containers will do the job) and lightly spray them with baking spray. Always choose non-fat baking sprays when preparing these chocolate protein bars. Divide the mixture into eight equal parts and fill the containers. Leave in the refrigerator overnight. If you like, you can sprinkle some more sweetener on top of your protein bars.

Nutritional values:

Carbohydrates 10.2g

Sugar 5.9g

Protein 12.2 g

Total fat (good monounsaturated fat) 11.6g

Sodium 123.8 mg

Potassium 85mg

Calcium 45.5mg

Iron 0.33mg

Vitamins (vitamin A; B-6; B-12; C; D; D2; D3; K; Riboflavin; Niacin; Thiamin; K)

Calories 53

2. Vanilla pudding bars

Ingredients:

1.5 scoops of protein powder (vanilla)

1 cup of oat flakes

1 package of pudding (vanilla flavor)

2 cups of skimmed milk

Preparation:

Mix the ingredients until you get a sticky mass. It should take about few minutes. Cook briefly, about 3-4 minutes, on a low temperature. Pour the mixture into a glass or a metal protein bar containers. You should get 8 protein bars with this mixture. Refrigerate overnight.

Nutritional values:

Carbohydrates 35g

Sugar 6.74g

Protein 52g

Total fat (good monounsaturated fat) 1,38g

Sodium 376mg

Homemade Protein Bar Recipes to Accelerate Muscle Development for Weightlifting

Potassium 880mg

Calcium 684.7mg

Iron 1.31mg

Vitamins (Vitamin C; B-6; B-12; A-RAE; A-IU; E; D; D-D2+D3; K; Thianin; Riboflavin; Niacin)

Calories 257

3. Low-fat yogurt bars

Ingredients:

½ cup of low fat fresh cheese

2 cups of low-fat yogurt

4 scoops of whey protein (vanilla)

½ cups of oat flakes

Preparation:

Mix the ingredients in a blender. Put it in a freezer for about an hour. Cut into 8 protein bars and keep in a refrigerator. Your protein bars are ready to eat after 2-3 hours.

Nutritional values:

Carbohydrates 19g

Sugar 5,76g

Protein 27,5g

Total fat 3.3g

Sodium 268,7mg

Homemade Protein Bar Recipes to Accelerate Muscle Development for Weightlifting

Potassium 535,3mg

Calcium 456,6mg

Iron 0,73mg

Vitamins (Vitamin C total ascorbic acid; B-6; B-12; A-RAE; A-IU; E; D; D-D2+D3; K-phylloquinone; Thianin; Riboflavin; Niacin)

Calories 228

4. Cottage cheese bars

Ingredients:

1 cup of low fat creamy cottage cheese

4 scoops of protein powder (chocolate)

1 cup of barley flakes cereal

2 tbsp of honey

½ tsp of cinnamon

Preparation:

Put the cheese with protein powder, honey and cinnamon in a large bowl. Mix the ingredients with an electric mixer. Mix until you get a smooth mixture. Add the barley flakes and mix few more minutes. If your mixture is too thick, add a little water. Pour the mixture into previously greased pan and refrigerate for about an hour. Cut into 10 protein bars. They are now ready to eat.

Nutritional values:

Carbohydrates 21g

Sugar 8.58g

Homemade Protein Bar Recipes to Accelerate Muscle Development for Weightlifting

Protein 24g

Total fat 4g

Sodium 221,2mg

Potassium 361,1mg

Calcium 333.5mg

Iron 5.23mg

Vitamins (Vitamin C total ascorbic acid; B-6; B-12; Folate-DFE; A-RAE; A-IU; E-alpha-tocopherol; D; D-D2+D3; K-phylloquinone; Thianin; Riboflavin; Niacin)

Calories 190

5. Protein bars of coconut and vanilla

Ingredients:

1 scoop of vanilla protein powder

1/4 cup coconut flakes

1/4 cup chopped coconut

1/4 cup milk (skimmed)

3 tbsp of melted dark chocolate (85% of cocoa)

Preparation:

Soak the coconut peaces into water and let it stand for about an hour. Meanwhile, mix the vanilla protein powder and coconut flakes with milk. You have to use skimmed milk. This significantly influences the nutritional value of your protein bars. The electric mixer will do the job. Now add chopped coconut peaces and mix well. Pour the mixture into a small pan and sprinkle with melted chocolate. Let it stand in the refrigerator for few hours. Cut into 3 large protein bars.

Nutritional values:

Carbohydrates 20g

Homemade Protein Bar Recipes to Accelerate Muscle Development for Weightlifting

Sugar 9.53g

Protein 19.25g

Total fat 6.06g

Sodium 53mg

Potassium 353mg

Calcium 302mg

Iron 12,6

Vitamins (Vitamin C total ascorbic acid; B-6; B-12; Folate-DFE; A-RAE; A-IU; E-alpha-tocopherol; D; D-D2+D3; K-phylloquinone; Thianin; Riboflavin; Niacin)

Calories 256

6. Protein bars with orange and goji berries

Ingredients:

1 scoop of organic protein powder (tasteless)

3/4 cup of ground almonds

1/4 cup of grated coconut

3/4 cup of goji berries

1 cup of coconut milk

½ glass of water

1 tsp of vanilla extract

1 tsp of grated orange peel

1 tsp of chili powder

3 tbsp of grated dark chocolate with 85% of cocoa

Preparation:

This recipe will give you 5 super healthy protein bars. First you need to mix the grated orange peel with chili, vanilla extract and coconut milk. Cook on a low temperature for 10-15 minutes. Allow it to cool. Meanwhile, mix the protein powder, almonds, grated coconut, goji berries and

Homemade Protein Bar Recipes to Accelerate Muscle Development for Weightlifting

water in a blender for few minutes. Add the cooled mixture of chili, vanilla extract, orange peel and coconut milk and mix for another 1-2 minutes. Pour the mixture into 8 protein bar containers and sprinkle with dark chocolate on top. Let it stand in the refrigerator for few hours.

Nutritional values:

Carbohydrates 14.5g

Sugar 2.61g

Protein 13.5g

Total fat 16.6 g

Sodium 49,5mg

Potassium 331mg

Calcium 121,8mg

Iron 37.6mg

Vitamins (Vitamin C; B-6; B-12; A-RAE; D; D-D2+D3; K-phylloquinone; Thianin; Riboflavin; Niacin)

Calories 248.8 kcal

7. Protein bars with pumpkin seeds

Ingredients:

2 small cooked carrots

1/2 cup of protein powder - vanilla

1/4 cup of minced pumpkin seeds

1/4 cup of skimmed milk

1 tsp of pumpkin seeds butter

2 tbsp of brown sugar

¼ cup of water

Preparation:

Wash and peel the carrots. Cut into smaller pieces and let it boil for about 20 minutes (until they are completely cooked). Allow it to cool. Melt the pumpkin seeds butter and add sugar. Mix well for few seconds. Then add milk and protein powder. Cook this mixture for few minutes (3-4 minutes) and add carrots. Mash until smooth, adding water constantly. Divide the mixture into 4 medium containers and sprinkle with minced pumpkin seeds. Let it stand in refrigerator for few hours.

Homemade Protein Bar Recipes to Accelerate Muscle Development for Weightlifting

Nutritional values:

Carbohydrates 21g

Sugar 7,93g

Protein 17.5

Total fat 9.3g

Sodium 52,3mg

Potassium 289mg

Calcium 127,6mg

Iron 12,3mg

Vitamins (Vitamin C total ascorbic acid; B-6; B-12; Folate-DFE; A-RAE; A-IU; E-alpha-tocopherol; D; D-D2+D3; K-phylloquinone; Thianin)

Calories 200

8. Orange juice protein bars

Ingredients:

3½ cups of oatmeal

1½ cups of milk powder (1.5% fat)

4 tbsp of protein powder (any flavor you like)

1 cup of honey

2 beaten egg whites

1 cup of orange juice

1 tsp of cinnamon

Preparation:

Sprinkle a baking pan with some low fat baking spray. Mix oatmeal, powdered milk and protein powder in a bowl. In a separate bowl, combine egg whites, orange juice and honey. Stir the liquid mixture into the dry. The mixture should be thick and similar to cookies dough. Pour the mixture into the baking pan and bake in preheated oven, at 350 degrees for 10-15 minutes. The edges should be crispy and brown. Cut into 10 pieces and allow it to cool. Leave in a refrigerator overnight

Homemade Protein Bar Recipes to Accelerate Muscle Development for Weightlifting

Nutritional values:

Carbohydrates 18.7g

Sugar 3.2g

Protein 17.5g

Total fat 14.8 g

Sodium 51,5mg

Potassium 328mg

Calcium 126,8mg

Iron 29.2mg

Vitamins (Vitamin C; B-6; B-12; A-RAE; D; D-D2+D3; K-phylloquinone; Thianin; Riboflavin; Niacin)

Calories 248.8 kcal

9. Coconut protein bars

Ingredients:

1 tip full scoop of vanilla protein powder

2 tip full scoops of coconut flour

½ cup of milk

2 large cubes of dark chocolate (80% of cocoa)

Preparation:

This is super easy recipe and it should take no more than 10 minutes. You will have very tasty protein bars. Mix the protein powder with coconut flour and pour milk. You should get a compact mixture. If it's too thick for your taste, add some water. You can't go wrong with this recipe. If you overdo with liquid, add dry ingredients, and vice versa. When you're finished, make 3 protein bars with this mixture and leave them in the refrigerator to squeeze slightly. Meanwhile, prepare the chocolate coating by melting the chocolate on a low temperature. Spread the chocolate over the protein bars and leave in the refrigerator for few hours.

Nutritional values:

Homemade Protein Bar Recipes to Accelerate Muscle Development for Weightlifting

Carbohydrates 14.5g

Sugar 2.61g

Protein 13.5g

Total fat 16.6 g

Sodium 49,5mg

Potassium 331mg

Calcium 121,8mg

Iron 37.6mg

Vitamins (Vitamin C total ascorbic acid; B-6; B-12; A-RAE; A-IU; E; D; D-D2+D3; K-phylloquinone; Thianin; Riboflavin; Niacin)

Calories 176.8 kcal

10. Almond protein bars

Ingredients:

¼ cup of grated almonds,

¼ cup of skimmed almond milk

¼ cup of freshly ground flax seeds

½ cup of coconut flower

3 egg whites

½ tsp of salt

¼ cup of almond butter

1 tbsp of honey

organic vanilla extract

½ cup of raisins

Preparation:

Mix the almonds, flax seeds, coconut flower, salt and egg whites in a food processor. Melt the almond butter until nice golden color and add honey, milk and vanilla extract. Let it cook for few minutes. Add the mixture of almonds, flax seeds, coconut flower, salt and eggs and let it boil.

Homemade Protein Bar Recipes to Accelerate Muscle Development for Weightlifting

Then add the raisins. Let it cool in a freezer for about an hour. Cut into 8 protein bars and leave in the refrigerator overnight.

Nutritional values:

Carbohydrates 21.8g

Sugar 8.61g

Protein 18.3g

Total fat 14.6 g

Sodium 54,5mg

Potassium 327mg

Calcium 112,8mg

Iron 25.3mg

Vitamins (Vitamin C; B-6; B-12; A-RAE; D; D-D2+D3; K-phylloquinone; Thianin; Riboflavin; Niacin)

Calories 232.7 kcal

11. Chocolate muesli protein bars

Ingredients:

3 cups of oatmeal

1 cup of chocolate muesli

½ cup of grated almonds

½ cup of grated hazelnuts

one cup of prunes, cut into small pieces (raisins, figs or Optional),

½ cup of peanuts,

2 tbsp of cocoa powder

4 scoops of chocolate protein powder

2 glasses of skimmed milk

Preparation:

Mix the ingredients in a large bowl until the mixture hardens. You can use an electric mixer for this. Pour the mixture into a baking pan and bake for about 30 minutes in preheated oven (350 degrees). It should get a nice golden brown color. Then remove it from the oven and cut into 8 protein bars. Let it stand for few hours. Your protein bars are ready to eat.

Nutritional values:

Carbohydrates 21.3g

Sugar 8.2g

Protein 19.4g

Total fat 13.4g

Sodium 52mg

Potassium 345mg

Calcium 133,2mg

Iron 23.6mg

Vitamins (Vitamin C; B-6; B-12; A-RAE; D; D-D2+D3; K-phylloquinone; Thianin; Riboflavin; Niacin)

Calories 239 kcal

12. Cranberries protein bars

Ingredients:

3 cups of oatmeal

½ cup of almonds

1 cup of dried cranberries

4 tbsp of peanut butter

1 glass of skimmed milk

4 scoops of vanilla protein powder

Preparation:

Mix the oatmeal, almonds and cranberries in a bowl. Melt the peanut butter on a low temperature. You want to add some milk before it melts – this way the peanut butter won't burn. When the peanut butter melts, add vanilla protein powder and let it boil. Remove from heat and allow it to cool. Now add the dry mixture and stir well. Pour the mixture into 5 protein bar containers and leave in the refrigerator. After about 4 hours, your protein bars are finished and ready to eat.

Nutritional values:

Homemade Protein Bar Recipes to Accelerate Muscle Development for Weightlifting

Carbohydrates 19.6g

Sugar 7.9g

Protein 19.3g

Total fat 12.3 g

Sodium 51,5mg

Potassium 298mg

Calcium 147mg

Iron 23.6mg

Vitamins (Vitamin C; B-6; B-12; A-RAE; D; D-D2+D3; K-phylloquinone, Thlanin; Riboflavin; Niacin)

Calories 224 kcal

13. Protein bars with coconut and lemon

Ingredients:

1 cup of chopped almonds or almond slices

1.5 cups of raisins

1 cup unsweetened coconut milk

1 tbsp of lemon zest

2 tbsp of lemon juice

Preparation:

Put all the ingredients into a blender. You want to soak the raisins in water for five minutes before you put them in a blender. Fill 5 protein bar containers with this mixture and leave in a freezer for about an hour. And that's it! Your protein bars are ready.

Nutritional values:

Carbohydrates 14.3g

Sugar 2,9g

Protein 14.9g

Total fat 13g

Sodium 29mg

Potassium 361mg

Calcium 112mg

Iron 13.6mg

Vitamins (Vitamin C; B-6; B-12; A-RAE; D; D-D2+D3; K-phylloquinone; Thianin; Riboflavin; Niacin)

Calories 200 kcal

14. Simple protein bars

Ingredients:

2 scoops of Whey protein powder

1 cup of organic oatmeal

1 glass of skimmed milk

4 tbsp of peanut butter

4 tbsp of honey

1 tbsp of cocoa powder

½ cup of freshly crushed flaxseed

Preparation:

Bind the Whey protein powder and cocoa powder with milk. Add honey and oatmeal. You want to stir well to get a dough-like mixture. Melt the peanut butter in a frying pan and fry crushed flax seeds for about 5 minutes. Remove from pan and add to the mixture. Pour the dough like mixture into the baking pan and sprinkle with flax seeds. Bake at 350 degrees, in preheated oven, for 10 minutes. Allow it to cool for a while and cut into 4 protein bars. Leave in the refrigerator overnight.

Homemade Protein Bar Recipes to Accelerate Muscle Development for Weightlifting

Nutritional values:

Carbohydrates 19g

Sugar 4.6g

Protein 18.5g

Total fat 12.2 g

Sodium 52mg

Potassium 401mg

Calcium 117mg

Iron 19.6mg

Vitamins (Vitamin C; B-6; B-12; A-RAE; D; D-D2+D3; K-phylloquinone; Thianin; Riboflavin; Niacin)

Calories 224 kcal

Homemade Protein Bar Recipes to Accelerate Muscle Development for Weightlifting

15. Almond butter protein bars

Ingredients:

1 cup of almond butter

3 tbsp of vanilla protein powder

½ cup of maple syrup

2 egg whites

2 cups of oatmeal

½ cup of grated coconut

1 tsp of baking powder

Preparation:

Use electric mixer to mix almond butter, protein powder and maple syrup. Add egg whites. Stir in the oatmeal, coconut and baking powder. Make a dough with this mixture. Pour it into a baking pan and bake in a preheated oven for about 10 minutes. It should have a nice light brown color. Allow it to cool well and cut into 4 protein bars. Keep them in a sealed bowl.

Nutritional values:

Homemade Protein Bar Recipes to Accelerate Muscle Development for Weightlifting

Carbohydrates 19g

Sugar 5.2g

Protein 17.3g

Total fat 12g

Sodium 51.1mg

Potassium 212mg

Calcium 114mg

Iron 22mg

Vitamins (Vitamin C; B-6; B-12; A-RAE; D; D-D2+D3; K-phylloquinone; Thianin; Riboflavin; Niacin)

Calories 217 kcal

16. Muesli chocolate bars

Ingredients:

1.5 cups quinoa flakes

½ cup of chopped walnuts

¼ cup of unsweetened, shredded coconut

¼ cup of sweetened vanilla protein powder

1 egg

2/3 cup of Greek yogurt

1/3 cup unsweetened almond butter

3 tbsp of honey

2 tbsp of melted coconut oil

1 tbsp of lemon peel

½ cup of raisins

Preparation:

Preheat oven to 350 degrees. Grease the baking pan with coconut oil. Spread evenly quinoa flakes, chopped walnuts and shredded coconut and bake for about 6-8 minutes.

Homemade Protein Bar Recipes to Accelerate Muscle Development for Weightlifting

Meanwhile, mix the Greek yogurt with egg, melted almond butter, honey, lemon peel and raisins. Remove the nuts from the oven and allow them to cool. Mix with Greek yogurt and pour into 12 protein bar containers. Leave it in a freezer for 3-4 hours and after that, keep your protein bars in the refrigerator.

Nutritional values:

Carbohydrates 20g

Sugar 5g

Protein 11g

Total fat 12g

Sodium 45mg

Potassium 209mg

Calcium 109mg

Iron 16mg

Vitamins (Vitamin C total ascorbic acid; B-6; B-12; Folate-DFE; A-RAE; A-IU; E-alpha-tocopherol; D; D-D2+D3; K-phylloquinone; Thianin)

Calories 227

17. Fruit protein bars

Ingredients:

1 cup of mixed dried fruit

1 cup of water

1.5 cup of oatmeal

1 cup of vanilla protein powder

3 tbsp of skimmed milk

2 tsp of grated lemon peel or orange

Preparation:

Soak the dried fruit in water and let it stand for 10-15 minutes. Use electric mixer to mix the oatmeal with protein powder and milk. Spread the mixture over a baking sheet. Coat with dried fruit, sprinkle with lemon/orange peel and bake for 10 minutes at 350 degrees. Allow it to cool and cut into 5 protein bars. Put them in the fridge for 30 minutes and your protein bars are ready to eat.

Nutritional values:

Carbohydrates 41g

Homemade Protein Bar Recipes to Accelerate Muscle Development for Weightlifting

Sugar 23g

Protein 17g

Total fat 3g

Sodium 36mg

Potassium 213mg

Calcium 145mg

Iron 12mg

Vitamins (Vitamin C total ascorbic acid; B-6; B-12; Folate-DFE; A-RAE; A-IU; E-alpha-tocopherol; D; D-D2+D3; K-phylloquinone; Thianin)

Calories 252

18. Protein bars with cranberries and orange

Ingredients:

1 cup of grated walnuts

½ cup of walnut butter

1.5 cups of skimmed milk

1.5 cups of vanilla protein powder

1/3 cup of dried cranberries

2 tsp of grated orange peel

Preparation:

Use the ingredients to make a smooth mixture in a blender. Pour the mixture into a baking pan, greased with walnut butter. Leave it like that in the refrigerator overnight. Cut into 8 equal protein bars and keep in the fridge.

Nutritional values:

Carbohydrates 41g

Sugar 23g

Protein 17g

Homemade Protein Bar Recipes to Accelerate Muscle Development for Weightlifting

Total fat 3g

Sodium 23mg

Potassium 222mg

Calcium 118,4mg

Iron 31mg

Vitamins (Vitamin C total ascorbic acid; B-6; B-12; Folate-DFE; A-RAE; A-IU; E-alpha-tocopherol; D; D-D2+D3; K-phylloquinone; Thianin)

Calories 252

19. Peanut butter protein bars

Ingredients:

2 cups of oat flakes

4 scoop of protein powder

5 tablespoons of peanut butter

1/2 cup milk

Preparation:

Another super easy recipe. All you need to do is mix the ingredients in a blender and pour into protein bar containers. With this mixture, you will get 5 protein bars. Leave in the refrigerator for few hours. They are now ready to eat!

Nutritional values:

Carbohydrates 16g

Sugar 7g

Protein 16g

Total fat 2.6g

Sodium 17mg

Potassium 212mg

Calcium 105,3mg

Iron 12mg

Vitamins (Vitamin C total ascorbic acid; B-6; B-12; Folate-DFE; A-RAE; A-IU; E-alpha-tocopherol; D; D-D2+D3; K-phylloquinone; Thianin)

Calories 167

20. Almond and vanilla protein bars

Ingredients:

½ cup of barley flakes

½ cup of protein powder

2 tbsp of peanut butter

4 tbsp of grated almonds

1 glass of a lukewarm water

Preparation:

Soak the flakes into lukewarm water for about 30 minutes. Melt the peanut butter on a low temperature, in a frying pan (you can add some water if it is easier – ¼ glass should do the trick). Fry the almonds for few minutes – just to get that nice golden color. Now add the soaked flakes and protein powder. Stir well for few minutes. Remove from the heat and allow it to cool for a while. Shape 5 protein bars with this mixture and leave it in the refrigerator overnight.

Nutritional values:

Carbohydrates 23g

Homemade Protein Bar Recipes to Accelerate Muscle Development for Weightlifting

Sugar 16g

Protein 19g

Total fat 2,8g

Sodium 39mg

Potassium 253mg

Calcium 129,9mg

Iron 33mg

Vitamins (Vitamin C total ascorbic acid; B-6; B-12; Folate-DFE; A-RAE; A-IU; E-alpha-tocopherol; D; D-D2+D3; K-phylloquinone; Thianin)

Calories 231

21. Protein bars with dried fruit

Ingredients:

2.5 cups of oatmeal

½ cup of almonds (peeled and roasted)

½ cup of hazelnuts (peeled and roasted)

1/3 cup of honey

1 cup of dried fruit (cranberries, apricots and yellow raisins)

1 cup of sugar free apple sauce

½ teaspoon of cinnamon

Preparation:

Chop the almonds and hazelnuts into larger pieces. Dried fruits also. Use a smaller baking pan and sprinkle it with low-fat baking spray. Bake the nuts and fruits in preheated oven for about 15 minutes at 350 degrees. Remove from the oven and allow it to cool for a while. Meanwhile, mix the cinnamon, apple sauce and honey with oatmeal. You want to use a blender for this. It should take about a minute.

Homemade Protein Bar Recipes to Accelerate Muscle Development for Weightlifting

Remove the nuts and fruits from the pan. Pour the mixture in it and top with the nuts. Bake for about 5 more minutes. Remove from the oven and leave it for few hours to cool. Cut into 20 protein bars and leave in the refrigerator overnight.

Nutritional values:

Carbohydrates 32,2g

Sugar 17g

Protein 19.9g

Total fat 5.6g

Sodium 31mg

Potassium 232,7mg

Calcium 126,4mg

Iron 27mg

Vitamins (Vitamin C total ascorbic acid; B-6; B-12; Folate-DFE; A-RAE; A-IU; E-alpha-tocopherol; D; D-D2+D3; K-phylloquinone; Thianin)

Calories 234

22. Amaranth Protein Bars

Ingredients:

1 cup of amaranth

3 tbsp of oats

3 tbsp of dried goji berries

3 tbsp of dried cranberries

1 tbsp of sesame

1 tbsp of sunflower seeds

2 tbsp of honey

1 large banana

1 tbsp of brown sugar

½ tsp of cinnamon

1 tbsp of oil

Preparation:

First you want to make amaranth popcorn. The procedure is the same as with regular popcorn. Use a frying pan and sprinkle some oil on it. Put the amaranth seeds in it and

Homemade Protein Bar Recipes to Accelerate Muscle Development for Weightlifting

fry for 10 minutes. You want to shake the frying pan several times, until the amaranth seeds are all cracked. Remove from heat and let it stand for a while.

Meanwhile, cut banana into smaller pieces. Mix with honey and other ingredients in a blender. If a mixture is too thick, the trick is to put it in a microwave for a minute. This will be enough to get a smooth mixture. Pour the mixture into baking pan, top with amaranth popcorn and bake in preheated oven for 5-10 minutes at 350 degrees. Remove from the oven, allow it to cool for a while and cut into 20 protein bars. Leave it in the refrigerator overnight.

Nutritional values:

Carbohydrates 41g

Sugar 25,1g

Protein 23,4g

Total fat 12g

Sodium 43mg

Potassium 217mg

Calcium 124,7mg

Iron 38mg

Homemade Protein Bar Recipes to Accelerate Muscle Development for Weightlifting

Vitamins (Vitamin C total ascorbic acid; B-6; B-12; Folate-DFE; A-RAE; A-IU; E-alpha-tocopherol; D; D-D2+D3; K-phylloquinone; Thianin)

Calories 278

23. Protein bars with sesame

Ingredients:

1.5 cup of brown sugar

1 lemon

¾ cup of sesame

Preparation:

Melt the sugar on a low temperature until you get a light brown caramel. Stir well and slowly pour the lemon juice in it. Now add sesame and mix well. Use a warm mixture to pour into protein bar containers. You should get 5 protein bars with this recipe. Allow it to cool in the refrigerator for several hours.

Nutritional values:

Carbohydrates 18g

Sugar 9g

Protein 14g

Total fat 2g

Sodium 16mg

Homemade Protein Bar Recipes to Accelerate Muscle Development for Weightlifting

Potassium 87mg

Calcium 8mg

Iron 7,1mg

Vitamins (Vitamin C; B-6; B-12; D; D-D2+D3;K)

Calories 112

24. Mediterranean corny with carob

Ingredients:

½ cup of oat flakes

3 tbsp of carob powder

2 tbsp of honey

1 tsp of cinnamon

pinch of salt

1 egg white, beaten in the firm snow

3 tbsp of mixed dried fruit

2 tbsp of orange juice

2 tbsp of plum jam

Preparation:

This recipe should give you 6 large protein bars. Mix well all the ingredients in a blender. Use a baking sheet and put it in a baking pan. Pour the mixture in it and bake for about 15 to 20 minutes in preheated oven at 250 degrees. Remove from heat, cut into 6 pieces and allow it to cool.

Nutritional values:

Homemade Protein Bar Recipes to Accelerate Muscle Development for Weightlifting

Carbohydrates 39g

Sugar 17,5g

Protein 29g

Total fat 9.4g

Sodium 39mg

Potassium 249mg

Calcium 128mg

Iron 32mg

Vitamins (Vitamin C total ascorbic acid; B-6; B-12; Folate-DFE; A-RAE; A-IU; E-alpha-tocopherol; D; D-D2+D3; K-phylloquinone; Thianin)

Calories 240

25. Sesame cubes

Ingredients:

1.5 cup of honey

1.5 cup of dark chocolate

½ cup of almond butter

1.5 cup of corn flakes

1.5 cup of sesame

1 tbsp of sesame oil

½ cup of lukewarm water

Preparation:

First you want to fry sesame seeds. Sprinkle some sesame oil on it, stir well and fry for few minutes. Seeds have to keep that light golden color. Remove from frying pan and leave it to cool.

Use a large bowl and a fork to crush corn flakes. Mix with sesame seeds, pour lukewarm water and let it stand for a while to soak the water.

Homemade Protein Bar Recipes to Accelerate Muscle Development for Weightlifting

Meanwhile, melt the almond butter on a low temperature. Add chocolate and honey and let it melt, stirring constantly. Remove from the heat.

Use a medium baking pen and pour the sesame seeds mixture in it. Coat with melted chocolate and cut into 8 pieces. Keep in the freezer for 2-3 hours. Remove from the freezer and keep your protein bars in the refrigerator.

Nutritional values:

Carbohydrates 41,8g

Sugar 26g

Protein 19g

Total fat 5,6g

Sodium 29mg

Potassium 249mg

Calcium 118,4mg

Iron 41mg

Vitamins (Vitamin C total ascorbic acid; B-6; B-12; Folate-DFE; A-RAE; A-IU; E-alpha-tocopherol; D; D-D2+D3; K-phylloquinone; Thianin)

Calories 239

26. Energy bars

Ingredients:

1 cup of oat flakes

4 tbsp of sunflower seeds

1/3 cup of almond flakes

2 tbsp of wheat seeds

½ cup of floral honey

3 tbsp of brown sugar

2 tbsp of peanut butter

1 tbsp of vanilla extract

pinch of salt

1 cup of chopped dried fruit (apricots, cherries, cranberries, raisins)

Preparation:

Mix the oat flakes, sunflower seeds, almond flakes and wheat seeds. Bake in preheated oven for 5-10 minutes. You can extend the baking time if you want them to be more crunchy, just don't overdo it.

Homemade Protein Bar Recipes to Accelerate Muscle Development for Weightlifting

Melt the sugar on a low temperature in a frying pan. Add honey, peanut butter, vanilla extract and salt. Stir well for few minutes. If the mixture is too thick, you can add some water (1/4 of a glass should do the trick). Pour the seeds in the frying pan and mix well. Divide the mixture into 10 equal pieces and coat with dried fruit. Leave in the refrigerator for few hours.

Nutritional values:

Carbohydrates 38,4g

Sugar 17,1g

Protein 27,9g

Total fat 12g

Sodium 39mg

Potassium 298mg

Calcium 112mg

Iron 29mg

Vitamins (Vitamin C total ascorbic acid; B-6; B-12; Folate-DFE; A-RAE; A-IU; E-alpha-tocopherol; D; D-D2+D3; K-phylloquinone; Thianin)

Calories 217

27. Quinoa & banana protein bars

Ingredients:

4 tbsp of quinoa

1 cup of oat flakes

1 egg

1 tbsp of honey

1 tbsp of olive oil

tsp cinnamon

pinch of salt

½ cup of raisins

1/3 cup of chopped hazelnuts

2 tbsp of sesame seeds

2 medium bananas

Preparation:

Cook quinoa for 10-15 minutes. Drain well and allow it to cool. Meanwhile mash the banana with a fork. Use a large

Homemade Protein Bar Recipes to Accelerate Muscle Development for Weightlifting

bowl to mix oat flakes, cinnamon, egg and salt. Add the drained quinoa to the mixture.

Sprinkle olive oil in a frying pan and add hazelnuts and sesame seeds. Fry on a low temperature for 5-10 minutes. Stir well and remove from the heat.

Pour the quinoa mixture in a medium baking pan. Make the second layer with hazelnuts and sesame seeds and coat with raisins. Bake at 350 degrees for about 10 minutes. You should get a nice brown color, or check with a toothpick. Remove from the oven, cut into 10 equal pieces and allow it to cool.

Nutritional values:

Carbohydrates 38,4g

Sugar 17,1g

Protein 27,9g

Total fat 12g

Sodium 39mg

Potassium 298mg

Calcium 112mg

Iron 29mg

Homemade Protein Bar Recipes to Accelerate Muscle Development for Weightlifting

Vitamins (Vitamin C total ascorbic acid; B-6; B-12; Folate-DFE; A-RAE; A-IU; E-alpha-tocopherol; D; D-D2+D3; K-phylloquinone; Thianin)

Calories 150

28. Rice protein bars

Ingredients:

½ cup of sesame seeds

1.5 cup of oat flakes

1 cup of peanut butter

1.5 cup of dark chocolate (80% of cocoa)

1 cup of rice crunchies

2 cups of mixed dried fruit

½ cup of minced walnuts

1 cup of honey

Preparation:

Bake sesame seeds in preheated oven, at 350 degrees for about 10 minutes to get a nice golden color. Remove from the oven and allow it to cool. Add the oat flakes and mix well.

Mix the chocolate, peanut butter and honey and melt it in a microwave (2-3 minutes will be enough).

Homemade Protein Bar Recipes to Accelerate Muscle Development for Weightlifting

Now you will need a medium sized baking pan. You will make three layers – first pour the oat flakes and sesame seeds. Make another layer with melted chocolate, honey and peanut butter. Coat with rice crunchies, minced walnut and dried fruit.

Bake at 350 degrees for another 5-10 minutes. Remove from the oven and allow it to cool. Cut into 10 protein bars and leave in the refrigerator for few hours.

Nutritional values:

Carbohydrates 38,9g

Sugar 25g

Protein 23g

Total fat 6,5g

Sodium 29,3mg

Potassium 259mg

Calcium 113,7mg

Iron 29mg

Vitamins (Vitamin C total ascorbic acid; B-6; B-12; Folate-DFE; A-IU; E-alpha-tocopherol; D; D-D2+D3; K-phylloquinone; Thianin)

Homemade Protein Bar Recipes to Accelerate Muscle Development for Weightlifting

Calories 249

29. Coco-banana protein bars

Ingredients:

3 large bananas

6 egg whites

1 cup of coconut milk

½ cup of shredded coconut

2 tsp of vanilla extract

2 tbsp of honey

Preparation:

These protein bars are super easy to prepare. All you need is a blender. Mix the ingredients in the blender for few minutes, or until you get a smooth mixture. Pour the mixture into protein bar containers and leave in the freezer for few hours. Remove from the freezer and keep in the refrigerator.

Carbohydrates 19.8g

Sugar 4.2g

Protein 18.6g

Homemade Protein Bar Recipes to Accelerate Muscle Development for Weightlifting

Total fat 11.8 g

Sodium 51,5mg

Potassium 328mg

Calcium 126,8mg

Iron 29.2mg

Vitamins (Vitamin C total ascorbic acid; B-6; B-12; A-RAE; A-IU; E; D; D-D2+D3; K-phylloquinone; Thianin; Riboflavin; Niacin)

Calories 222.8 kcal

30. Chili protein bars

Ingredients:

1 cup of coconut flour

3 egg whites

1 glass of almond milk

1 tbsp of honey

1 tsp of chili

1 tbsp of cocoa

5 tbsp of grated dark chocolate (80% of cocoa)

½ glass of coconut milk

Preparation:

Place coconut flour, egg whites, almond milk, honey and chili in a food processor. Process until you get a smooth mixture. Bake the mixture in preheated oven at 350 degrees for about 10-15 minutes. Remove from the oven and cut into 5 equal protein bars.

Homemade Protein Bar Recipes to Accelerate Muscle Development for Weightlifting

Meanwhile boil the coconut milk and add cocoa and chocolate. Cook for 2-3 minutes and remove from heat. Allow it to cool for a while.

Now you want to soak the protein bars into the chocolate mixture. Leave them in the chocolate for 15-20 minutes. Keep your protein bars in the refrigerator.

Nutritional values:

Carbohydrates 17.8g

Sugar 5.2g

Protein 16g

Total fat 9g

Sodium 45,9mg

Potassium 342mg

Calcium 113mg

Iron 21.2mg

Vitamins (Vitamin C; B-6; B-12; A-RAE; D; D-D2+D3; K-phylloquinone; Thianin; Riboflavin; Niacin)

Calories 234 kcal

31. Greek yogurt protein bars

Ingredients:

1 cup of Greek yogurt

1 large banana

3 egg whites

½ cup of minced walnuts

1 tsp of vanilla extract

½ cup of coconut flour

1 tbsp of brown sugar

½ cup of cranberries

½ cup of minced hazelnuts

Preparation:

Mix the Greek yogurt with banana, egg whites, minced walnuts and vanilla in a food processor. You want to make a smooth mixture. Leave that mixture in the refrigerator for at least an hour. Remove from the refrigerator, make 8 protein bars. Coat them with cranberries, brown sugar and hazelnuts and roll into coconut flour. Bake on a baking sheet, in preheated oven at 350 degrees for 10 minutes. Remove from the oven and allow it to cool. Keep them in the refrigerator.

Nutritional values:

Carbohydrates 21.9g

Sugar 9.7g

Protein 19.5g

Total fat 15g

Sodium 46,3mg

Potassium 312mg

Calcium 148mg

Iron 30mg

Vitamins (Vitamin C; B-6; B-12; A-RAE; D; D-D2+D3; K-phylloquinone; Thianin; Riboflavin; Niacin)

Calories 216 kcal

32. Apple juice protein bars

Ingredients:

1 cup of oatmeal

½ cup of flour

¼ cup of chopped almonds and hazelnuts

¼ cup of raisins

¼ cup of freshly squeezed apple juice

¼ cup of honey

½ tsp of cinnamon

2 tbsp of oil

1 tbsp of melted almond butter

Preparation:

Mix all the dry ingredients. Add oil, almond butter, apple juice and honey. Stir well to get a smooth mixture. Pour the mixture on a baking sheet. It should be about 0.5 inch thick. Bake in preheated oven at 250 degrees for 15-20 minutes. Remove from the oven, cut into 10 protein bars and let it stand in the refrigerator for few hours.

Homemade Protein Bar Recipes to Accelerate Muscle Development for Weightlifting

Nutritional values:

Carbohydrates 21g

Sugar 6g

Protein 19,3g

Total fat 12g

Sodium 49,5mg

Potassium 318mg

Calcium 112mg

Iron 23.2mg

Vitamins (Vitamin C; B-6; B-12; A-RAE; D; D-D2+D3; K-phylloquinone; Thianin; Riboflavin; Niacin)

Calories 212 kcal

33. Protein bars with figs

Ingredients:

1 cup of chopped almonds

¼ cup of chopped dried figs

¼ cup of chopped dried plums

¼ cup of raisins

2 tsp of cinnamon

2 tbsp of oat flakes

½ cup of almond milk

Preparation:

Mix the almonds, dried figs, plums, raisins, cinnamon and oat flakes in a food processor. Add milk and mix for another 1-2 minutes. Place this mixture on a baking sheet and bake in preheated oven at 225 degrees for about 45 minutes. The mixture must be very dry. Remove from the oven, cut into 10 protein bars and keep in a dry and cold place.

Homemade Protein Bar Recipes to Accelerate Muscle Development for Weightlifting

If it is easier for you, you can make protein bars before baking/drying. Use protein bars mold and shape the mixture with it.

Little secret: All those who have a dehydrator, use it for this recipe. It will preserve all the nutrients.

Nutritional values:

Carbohydrates 20g

Sugar 7,6g

Protein 19g

Total fat 12g

Sodium 58mg

Potassium 312mg

Calcium 140,2mg

Iron 23mg

Vitamins (Vitamin C; B-6; B-12; A-RAE; D; D-D2+D3; K-phylloquinone; Thianin; Riboflavin; Niacin)

Calories 219 kcal

34. Power mix protein bars

Ingredients:

2 large oranges

1 tbsp of light honey

3 tbsp of brown sugar

6 tbsp of almond butter

8 tbsp of maple syrup

2 tbsp of cranberries jam

3 tbsp of hazelnuts

3 tbsp of white almonds

2 tbsp of walnuts

2 tbsp of cracked amaranth

3 tbsp of golden raisins

10 tbsp of fine oat flakes

8 tbsp of grated dark chocolate (80% of cocoa)

Preparation:

Homemade Protein Bar Recipes to Accelerate Muscle Development for Weightlifting

Wash and dry the oranges. Finely peel the scrub. Squeeze the juice from the oranges, add sugar and honey and boil on a high temperature with constant stirring, until all the liquid evaporates. You will get a very thick jam.

Cut hazelnuts, almonds and walnuts into small pieces.

Mix the almond butter, maple syrup and cranberries jam by using an electric mixer. Put it in a microwave for 1-2 minutes. Remove from the microwave and mix with orange jam, nuts, amaranth and oats. You will get a very thick mixture. Keep it like that. Now you will need protein bar molds. Shape 10 protein bars and bake them in preheated oven for 10 minutes at 350 degrees. Remove from the oven and allow it to cool.

Melt the chocolate in the microwave for few minutes. Soak your protein bars into the chocolate and leave in the refrigerator for several hours.

Nutritional values:

Carbohydrates 28g

Sugar 11g

Protein 23g

Total fat 17.8 g

Homemade Protein Bar Recipes to Accelerate Muscle Development for Weightlifting

Sodium 58,3g

Potassium 369mg

Calcium 141mg

Iron 34mg

Vitamins (Vitamin C; B-6; B-12; A-RAE; D; D-D2+D3; K-phylloquinone; Thianin; Riboflavin; Niacin)

Calories 268.8 kcal

35. Apricot protein bars

Ingredients:

4 tbsp of brown sugar

3 tbsp of honey

4 tbsp of peanut butter

2 tbsp of freshly squeezed apricot juice

1 tbsp of grated orange zest

1 cup of rice flakes

½ cup of chopped apricots

½ cup of chopped walnuts

Preparation:

Combine all the ingredients in a large bowl. Use an electric mixer to get a homogeneous mass. Preheat the oven to 250 degrees. Pour the mixture on a baking sheet and bake for about 15 minutes. It should get golden brown color. Remove from the oven, cut into 5 protein bars and keep in a dry and cold place.

Nutritional values:

Homemade Protein Bar Recipes to Accelerate Muscle Development for Weightlifting

Carbohydrates 20.7g

Sugar 7.4g

Protein 19.5g

Total fat 13g

Sodium 49mg

Potassium 294mg

Calcium 112,8mg

Iron 27mg

Vitamins (Vitamin C; B-6; B-12; A-RAE; D; D-D2+D3; K-phylloquinone; Thianin; Riboflavin; Niacin)

Calories 259 kcal

Homemade Protein Bar Recipes to Accelerate Muscle Development for Weightlifting

36. Protein bars with mixed fruits

Ingredients:

¼ cup of chopped dried figs

¼ cup of chopped dates

¼ cup of sliced prunes

¼ cup of white raisins

¼ cup of chopped dried orange

¼ cup of chopped dried plums

1 glass of fresh orange juice

1 glass of fresh lemon juice

¼ cup of ground walnuts

¼ cup of ground hazelnuts

¼ cup of honey

a few drops of rum extract

¼ cup of chopped pineapple

1 cup of melted dark chocolate (80% of cocoa)

¼ cup of cocoa

Homemade Protein Bar Recipes to Accelerate Muscle Development for Weightlifting

¼ cup of almond butter

Preparation:

Mix well fruits, nuts, honey, orange and lemon juice in a large bowl. Keep the mixture in a bowl. Melt the almond butter on a low temperature, add rum extract, dark chocolate and cocoa. Keep cooking until the boiling point. Stir constantly! Remove from the heat and use this mixture to bind the fruit and nuts mixture. Mix well and shape 18 protein bars. Keep them in the refrigerator for several hours. These protein bars are very delicious and crunchy.

Nutritional values:

Carbohydrates 27g

Sugar 9g

Protein 23.8g

Total fat 17.8 g

Sodium 64mg

Potassium 417mg

Calcium 139mg

Iron 31mg

Homemade Protein Bar Recipes to Accelerate Muscle Development for Weightlifting

Vitamins (Vitamin C; B-6; B-12; A-RAE; D; D-D2+D3; K-phylloquinone; Thianin; Riboflavin; Niacin)

Calories 289kcal

37. Crispy protein bars

Ingredients:

½ cup of dried figs

¼ cup of dried coconut

¼ cup of roasted peanuts

¼ cup of wheat flakes

¼ cup of rice flakes

3 tbsp of roasted wheat

½ cup of honey

½ cup of peanut butter

3 tbsp of agave syrup

4 tbsp of brown sugar

¼ tsp of ground cinnamon

1 tsp of vanilla extract

Preparation:

Combine figs, dried coconut and roasted peanut in a large bowl. Add wheat, roasted wheat, rice and stir well.

Homemade Protein Bar Recipes to Accelerate Muscle Development for Weightlifting

In a smaller bowl, bind honey with peanut butter, agave syrup and brown sugar. Cook for several minutes on a low temperature until the brown sugar is fully dissolved. Add cinnamon, vanilla extract and bring it to the boiling point. Remove from the heat. Pour this mixture over the prepared nuts and fruits and mix well.

Use a medium sized baking sheet, put the mixture in it and bake for about 20 minutes at 225 degrees. Remove from the oven, cut into 24 protein bars and leave them in the refrigerator for at least few hours.

Nutritional values:

Carbohydrates 29g

Sugar 11,3g

Protein 26g

Total fat 11g

Sodium 61,1mg

Potassium 287mg

Calcium 134mg

Iron 31mg

Homemade Protein Bar Recipes to Accelerate Muscle Development for Weightlifting

Vitamins (Vitamin C; B-6; B-12; A-RAE; D; D-D2+D3; K-phylloquinone; Thianin; Riboflavin; Niacin)

Calories 254 kcal

38. Cottage cheese & blueberries protein bars

Ingredients:

1 cup of low fat cottage cheese

1 cup of Greek yogurt

2 egg whites

½ cup of blueberries

4 tbsp of brown sugar

1 tsp of vanilla extract

½ cup of coconut flour

Preparation:

Put all the ingredients, except coconut flour, into the food processor. Mix well to get a smooth mixture. Use protein bar mold to create 10 equal protein bars. Sprinkle them with coconut flour and freeze for few hours. Remove from the freezer and keep in the refrigerator.

Nutritional values:

Carbohydrates 18.7g

Sugar 5.2g

Homemade Protein Bar Recipes to Accelerate Muscle Development for Weightlifting

Protein 16.7g

Total fat 16.5 g

Sodium 54,7mg

Potassium 339mg

Calcium 138,5mg

Iron 24.8mg

Vitamins (Vitamin C; B-6; B-12; A-RAE; D; D-D2+D3; K-phylloquinone; Thianin; Riboflavin; Niacin)

Calories 236.7 kcal

Homemade Protein Bar Recipes to Accelerate Muscle Development for Weightlifting

39. Chia seeds protein bars

Ingredients:

1 cup of minced chia seeds

½ cup of walnuts

½ cup of hazelnuts

½ cup of cranberries

1 cup of low fat cheese

½ cup of honey

1 tbsp of vanilla extract

1 tsp of cinnamon

1 scoop of protein powder

low fat baking spray

Preparation:

Mix the chia seeds with nuts and cheese. Use protein bar molds to make 8 equal protein bars.

Homemade Protein Bar Recipes to Accelerate Muscle Development for Weightlifting

With an electric mixer, combine honey, cinnamon, vanilla extract and protein powder. Now you have to pour this mixture over the protein bars.

Preheat the oven at 350 degrees. Sprinkle the baking sheet with low fat baking spray and bake protein bars for about 20 minutes, until you get a light brown color. Remove from the oven and allow it to cool. Keep in the refrigerator for several hours.

Nutritional values:

Carbohydrates 14.9g

Sugar 5.3g

Protein 18.3g

Total fat 14.6 g

Sodium 52,7mg

Potassium 326mg

Calcium 127,3mg

Iron 26.3mg

Vitamins (Vitamin C; B-6; B-12; A-RAE; D; D-D2+D3; K-phylloquinone; Thianin; Riboflavin; Niacin)

Calories 226.3 kcal

40. Oatmeal protein bars

Ingredients:

1 cup of oatmeal

¼ cup of cornflakes

½ cup of crushed hazelnuts

6 - 8 pieces of prunes cut into cubes

1/3 cup of raisins

1/3 cup of sesame seeds

1/3 cup of flaxseed

½ cup of brown sugar

½ cup of grated chocolate (80% of cocoa)

1 medium sized orange

1 tsp of cinnamon

1 tsp of rum extract

½ cup of peanut butter

2 tbsp of honey

Homemade Protein Bar Recipes to Accelerate Muscle Development for Weightlifting

¼ cup of grated chocolate (80% of cocoa) – for decoration

Preparation:

Combine all dry ingredients in a large bowl. Wash the orange, grate the peel and squeeze it. Use a frying pan to melt the peanut butter on a low temperature. Add sugar, rum extract, cinnamon, rind and orange juice. Stir well and let it cook for 3-5 minutes. Then add the dry ingredients into the frying pan and stir well again. Add honey. Remove from the heat, allow it to cool for a while and make 15 equal protein bars. Decorate with some more chocolate and keep in the refrigerator overnight.

Nutritional values:

Carbohydrates 27.2g

Sugar 9.2g

Protein 26.3g

Total fat 12.8 g

Sodium 96,5mg

Potassium 356mg

Calcium 124,8mg

Iron 29.2mg

Homemade Protein Bar Recipes to Accelerate Muscle Development for Weightlifting

Vitamins (Vitamin C; B-6; B-12; A-RAE; D; D-D2+D3; K-phylloquinone; Thianin; Riboflavin; Niacin)

Calories 278.3 kcal

41. Honey protein bars

Ingredients:

½ cup of almond butter

½ cup of honey

2 eggs

1/3 cup of ground almonds

½ cup of dried apricots – cut into small pieces

¼ cup of roasted hazelnuts, finely chopped

¼ cup of dried cherries, finely chopped

¼ cup of sesame

1/3 cup of oats

1 tbsp of sesame oil

Preparation:

For this recipe, you will need a small baking sheet. Sprinkle some sesame oil over it.

Homemade Protein Bar Recipes to Accelerate Muscle Development for Weightlifting

Whisk the almond butter with honey until creamy mixture, then add the beaten eggs, nuts and fruits. Continue to whisk this mixture for few more minutes.

Preheat the oven at 350 degrees. Pour the mixture on a baking sheet and bake for about 20-25 minutes, until golden color. Remove from the oven and cool for about 10 minutes. Cut into 10 equal protein bars. You can add some more honey on top, but this is optional and increases the nutritional value. The good thing about these protein bars is that they are perfect warm as well as cold.

Nutritional values:

Carbohydrates 28.7g

Sugar 9.2g

Protein 27.5g

Total fat 14.8 g

Sodium 51,5mg

Potassium 328mg

Calcium 126,8mg

Iron 29.2mg

Homemade Protein Bar Recipes to Accelerate Muscle Development for Weightlifting

Vitamins (Vitamin C; B-6; B-12; A-RAE; D; D-D2+D3; K-phylloquinone; Thianin; Riboflavin; Niacin)

Calories 248.8 kcal

42. Protein bars with oatmeal and raisins

Ingredients:

½ cup of oat flakes

½ cup of chopped walnuts

½ cup of raisins

½ cup of chopped dry plums

½ cup of sunflower seeds

½ cup of melted coconut oil

¼ cup of chia seeds

¼ cup of honey

¼ cup of chocolate (70% of cocoa)

1 tsp of cinnamon

Preparation:

Preheat the oven at 350 degrees. Use a saucepan to melt the chocolate and coconut oil on a very low temperature. Stir well. Mix it with other ingredients in a large bowl. Spread the mixture on a baking sheet and bake for 15 minutes. Allow it to cool and keep in the refrigerator for few hours.

Nutritional values:

Carbohydrates 27.6g

Sugar 9.2g

Protein 25.3g

Total fat 15.8 g

Sodium 61,2mg

Potassium 229mg

Calcium 134,4mg

Iron 24.3mg

Vitamins (Vitamin C; B-6; B-12; A-RAE; D; D-D2+D3; K-phylloquinone; Thianin; Riboflavin; Niacin)

Calories 228 kcal

43. Protein bars with dates

Ingredients:

½ cup of chopped dates

¼ cup of chopped dried apricots

¼ cup of raisins

¼ cup of dried cranberries

1 tbsp of peanut butter

¼ tsp of ground cinnamon

5 tbsp of agave syrup

¼ cup of grated walnuts

¼ cup of grated almonds

Preparation:

Use an electric food processor to process dates, apricots, raisins and cranberries. Add the peanut butter, cinnamon, agave syrup and mix well. Pour this mixture on a baking sheet. Spread the walnuts and almonds on top of it and press a little bit with your hands. Cover with adhesive foil and place in the refrigerator for at least 3-4 hours. Cut into 10 equal protein bars.

Nutritional values:

Carbohydrates 23.4g

Sugar 5.2g

Protein 19.5g

Total fat 13.4 g

Sodium 41,4mg

Potassium 353mg

Calcium 135,5mg

Iron 19mg

Vitamins (Vitamin C; B-6; B-12; A-RAE; D; D-D2+D3; K-phylloquinone; Thianin; Riboflavin; Niacin)

Calories 236.6 kcal

44. Protein bars with pistachios

Ingredients:

1 cup of roasted pistachios – chopped into small pieces

1 cup of chopped dates

1 tsp of cocoa

1 tsp of cinnamon

2 tsp of vanilla sugar

1 lemon

pinch of salt

1 cup of mixed chopped dried fruit

Preparation:

Use an electric blender to mix dates and pistachios. Add other ingredients and mix for another few minutes. Use this mixture to create 10 protein bars. You can do it manually or you can use protein bar molds. Leave it in the refrigerator overnight.

Nutritional values:

Carbohydrates 19.7g

Homemade Protein Bar Recipes to Accelerate Muscle Development for Weightlifting

Sugar 7.4g

Protein 18.5g

Total fat 13.5 g

Sodium 31,8mg

Potassium 326mg

Calcium 124mg

Iron 23.2mg

Vitamins (Vitamin C; B-6; B-12; A-RAE; D; D-D2+D3; K-phylloquinone; Thianin; Riboflavin; Niacin)

Calories 243.7 kcal

45. Protein bars molasses

Ingredients:

½ cup of dark sugar syrup - molasses

¼ cup of peanut butter

½ cup of brown sugar

¼ cup of walnuts

¼ cup of chopped dried apricots

¼ cup of chopped dried figs

1 cup of oat flakes

¼ cup of pumpkin seeds

Preparation:

Preheat the oven at 350 degrees. Chop the walnuts into very small pieces. Use a saucepan to mix the peanut butter, sugar and sugar syrup. Cook it for about 5 minutes on a very low temperature. Stir well. Let it boil. The mixture should be moist and slightly sticky, not dry. Remove from the heat and mix with the walnuts, dried fruits, oat flakes and pumpkin seeds.

Homemade Protein Bar Recipes to Accelerate Muscle Development for Weightlifting

Bake for about 30 minutes. Allow it to cool for about an hour or even two before you cut it into 10 equal protein bars.

Nutritional values:

Carbohydrates 26.4g

Sugar 4.6g

Protein 19.5g

Total fat 12.2 g

Sodium 21,9mg

Potassium 368mg

Calcium 111mg

Iron 25.3mg

Vitamins (Vitamin C; B-6; B-12; A-RAE; D; D-D2+D3; K-phylloquinone; Thianin; Riboflavin; Niacin)

Calories 219 kcal

46. Protein bars with turmeric and raspberries

Ingredients:

½ cup of soy milk

1 cup of smashed banana

1 cup of coconut flour

½ cup of turmeric

2 egg whites

½ cup of grated walnuts

½ cup of raspberries

Preparation:

This recipe is very easy to prepare. It does not need any cooking or baking. All you need is a blender to mix all the ingredients for few minutes. Pour the mixture into protein bar molds and leave in the freezer for few hours. When finished, keep them in the refrigerator.

Nutritional values:

Carbohydrates 21.3g

Sugar 6.4g

Homemade Protein Bar Recipes to Accelerate Muscle Development for Weightlifting

Protein 19.5g

Total fat 11.4 g

Sodium 33,7mg

Potassium 343mg

Calcium 133mg

Iron 13.2mg

Vitamins (Vitamin C; B-6; B-12; A-RAE; D; D-D2+D3; K-phylloquinone; Thianin; Riboflavin; Niacin)

Calories 232.4 kcal

47. Protein bars with red pepper

Ingredients:

3 tbsp of cocoa powder

1.5 cup of almonds

½ cup of buckwheat flour

2 tsp of cinnamon

½ tsp of ground red pepper

½ cup of chopped chocolate (80% of cocoa)

1 cup of brown sugar

1 cup of honey

Preparation:

Preheat oven to 250 degrees. Mix the cocoa, chopped almonds, buckwheat flour, cinnamon and pepper in a large bowl. Use a saucepan to melt the chocolate, sugar and honey on a low temperature. Stir well and add the dry mixture to it. Mix well and remove from the heat. Allow it to cool for a while and make 10 protein bars with your hands or with the mold. Sprinkle them with some more cocoa powder, just for decoration. Bake for about

Homemade Protein Bar Recipes to Accelerate Muscle Development for Weightlifting

30 minutes. Remove from the oven, allow it to cool and keep in the refrigerator.

Nutritional values:

Carbohydrates 21g

Sugar 5.4g

Protein 19.3g

Total fat 12.3 g

Sodium 32,2mg

Potassium 236mg

Calcium 121mg

Iron 23,2mg

Vitamins (Vitamin C; B-6; B-12; A-RAE; D; D-D2+D3; K-phylloquinone; Thianin; Riboflavin; Niacin)

Calories 219 kcal

48. Protein bars with blackberries

Ingredients:

1 cup of blackberries

1 cup of cornflakes

1 cup of low fat cheese

1 tsp of blackberries extract

½ cup of rice flour

Preparation:

Another super easy recipe. Mix the ingredients with an electric mixer. Use protein bar molds to create 10 protein bars with this mixture. Preheat oven to 350 degrees and bake your protein bars for 15 minutes. Remove from the oven, allow it to cool for about an hour before you put it into the refrigerator.

Nutritional values:

Carbohydrates 19,1g

Sugar 3.4g

Protein 18.5g

Homemade Protein Bar Recipes to Accelerate Muscle Development for Weightlifting

Total fat 13.2 g

Sodium 35,2mg

Potassium 392mg

Calcium 121mg

Iron 21.3mg

Vitamins (Vitamin C; B-6; B-12; A-RAE; D; D-D2+D3; K-phylloquinone; Thianin; Riboflavin; Niacin)

Calories 211 kcal

49. Toffee protein bars

Ingredients:

½ cup of almond butter

½ cup of brown sugar

2 tbsp of maple syrup

1.5 cup of oat flakes

pinch of salt

Preparation:

Melt the almond butter and sugar on a low temperature. It should not boil, but it must have golden brown color. Add maple syrup and mix well for another minute. Remove from the heat, add salt and oat flakes. It will be a very sticky mixture.

Pour that mixture on a baking sheet and bake in preheated at 225 degrees, for 20-25 minutes. Remove from the oven, allow it to cool for about an hour, and cut into 6 equal protein bars. It is very important for the mixture to cool completely. Otherwise you will not be able to cut it properly. Keep them in the refrigerator.

Homemade Protein Bar Recipes to Accelerate Muscle Development for Weightlifting

Nutritional values:

Carbohydrates 21.7g

Sugar 5.4g

Protein 13.5g

Total fat 14.2 g

Sodium 32,4mg

Potassium 311mg

Calcium 133mg

Iron 21.4mg

Vitamins (Vitamin C; B-6; B-12; A-RAE; D; D-D2+D3; K-phylloquinone; Thianin; Riboflavin; Niacin)

Calories 212 kcal

50. Healthy cubes

Ingredients:

5 tbsp of almond butter

8 tbsp of brown sugar

3 tbsp of honey

4 tbsp of raisins

4 tbsp of grated hazelnuts

1 cup of oat flakes

3 tbsp of brown powdered sugar

2 tsp of lemon juice

Preparation:

Melt the almond butter on a low temperature and add honey and sugar. Fry for few minutes and stir well. Add raisins, grated hazelnuts and oat flakes. Stir well until you get a thick mixture. Pour the mixture into a baking pan, sprinkle with brown powdered sugar and lemon juice. Bake in preheated oven at 250 degrees for 15 minutes. You should get a nice brown color and a crunchy texture. It all depends on the thickness.

Homemade Protein Bar Recipes to Accelerate Muscle Development for Weightlifting

Remove from the oven, allow it to cool for a while and cut into 8 pieces. Your protein bars are finished. If desired, you can sprinkle some more lemon juice on top. A great tip for this recipe is to sprinkle some maple syrup on top. But this is optional. Leave in the refrigerator overnight.

Nutritional values:

Carbohydrates 37g

Sugar 16g

Protein 25,6g

Total fat 6g

Sodium 27mg

Potassium 245mg

Calcium 98mg

Iron 224mg

Vitamins (Vitamin C total ascorbic acid; B-6; B-12; Folate-DFE; A-RAE; A-IU; E-alpha-tocopherol; D; D-D2+D3; K-phylloquinone; Thianin)

Calories 239

OTHER GREAT TITLES BY THIS AUTHOR

The Ultimate Guide to Weight Training Nutrition: Maximize Your Potential

By Joseph Correa

Becoming Mentally Tougher In Bodybuilding by Using Meditation: Reach Your Potential by Controlling Your Inner Thoughts

By Joseph Correa

www.ingramcontent.com/pod-product-compliance
Lightning Source LLC
Chambersburg PA
CBHW070150080526
44586CB00015B/1925